POWER UP YOUR

Woo Woo

JOURNAL

Copyright © 2020 by Dianne Gebhardt

Power Up Your Woo Woo: 7 Steps to Personal Growth, Empowerment and Spiritual Healing with Tarot and Oracle Cards

All rights reserved. No part of this publication may be reproduced, distributed or transmitted in any form or by any means, including photocopying, recording, or other electronic or mechanical methods, without the prior written permission of the publisher, except in the case of brief quotations embodied in critical reviews and certain other noncommercial uses permitted by copyright law.

Although the author and publisher have made every effort to ensure that the information in this book was correct at press time, the author and publisher do not assume and hereby disclaim any liability to any party for any loss, damage, or disruption caused by errors or omissions, whether such errors or omissions result from negligence, accident, or any other cause.

Adherence to all applicable laws and regulations, including international, federal, state and local governing professional licensing, business practices, advertising, and all other aspects of doing business in the US, Canada or any other jurisdiction is the sole responsibility of the reader and consumer.

Neither the author nor the publisher assumes any responsibility or liability whatsoever on behalf of the consumer or reader of this material. Any perceived slight of any individual or organization is purely unintentional.

The resources in this book are provided for informational purposes only and should not be used to replace the specialized training and professional judgment of a health care or mental health care professional.

Neither the author nor the publisher can be held responsible for the use of the information provided within this book. Please always consult a trained professional before making any decision regarding treatment of yourself or others.

DianneGebhardt.com

ISBN: 978-1-7360872-3-7

JOURNAL

Dear Readers of *Power Up Your Woo Woo: 7 Steps to Personal Growth, Empowerment, and Spiritual Healing with Tarot and Oracle Cards* ~

Thank you from the bottom of my heart for your purchase of the book and the journal. It is my sincere hope that in using this journal, you will experience connecting with your Infinite Spiritual Team regularly and easily. You will gain guidance, comfort, support, and best of all so much love from your Team as you write and reflect here. You will grow personally and spiritually and feel more empowered through your card and journal work.

Within this journal, a reading template is provided for each week in a year. Space has also been provided for your question work and any other notes you would like to make. Thank you for purchasing both the
Power Up Your Woo Woo book and journal.

The Divine in me recognizes and honors the Divine in you.

Visit DianneGebhardt.com to download your free gift.

Please kindly use these links to go to Amazon and leave a review of the book and journal. Your reviews will help me revise these two items and also help me as I write and create new products.

NAMASTE, DIANNE GEBHARDT

"Every thought we think, every feeling we have, every word we speak goes out into the atmosphere to either heal or harm. Let us be healers. Let us be harmless."

—John R. Price

Invitation to Infinite Spiritual Team:	Date: / /

Intention:

Question:

- 4. Me Now / How I'm Showing Up in the World
- 1. New Beginnings / Creation
- 2. My Strength / Power
- 3. Manifestation / Flow

Takeaways:
1.

2.

3.

4.

Affirmations:

Action/Allowing:

Questions I Still Have:

Gratitude and Closing:

| Invitation to Infinite Spiritual Team: | Date: /   / |

Intention:

Question:

4. Me Now / How I'm Showing Up in the World

3. Manifestation / Flow

1. New Beginnings / Creation

2. My Strength / Power

Takeaways:
1.

2.

3.

4.

Affirmations:

Action/Allowing:

Questions I Still Have:

Gratitude and Closing:

"We must not allow our thinking to be governed by the conditions that surround us."

—U.S. Anderson

NOTES

Invitation to Infinite Spiritual Team:	Date: / /

Intention:

Question:

- 4. Me Now/ How I'm Showing Up in the World
- 1. New Beginnings/ Creation
- 2. My Strength/Power
- 3. Manifestation/Flow

Takeaways:
1.

2.

3.

4.

Affirmations:

Action/Allowing:

Questions I Still Have:

Gratitude and Closing:

| Invitation to Infinite Spiritual Team: | Date: / / |

Intention:

Question:

```
        4.
   Me Now/ How I'm
 Showing Up in the World

3.                              1.
Manifestation/Flow         New Beginnings/
                              Creation

        2.
   My Strength/Power
```

Takeaways:
1.

2.

3.

4.

Affirmations:

Action/Allowing:

Questions I Still Have:

Gratitude and Closing:

"Everything that is created begins in the mind."

—Ruth Fishel

| Invitation to Infinite Spiritual Team: | Date: /   / |

Intention:

Question:

- 4. Me Now/ How I'm Showing Up in the World
- 1. New Beginnings/ Creation
- 2. My Strength/Power
- 3. Manifestation/Flow

Takeaways:
1.

2.

3.

4.

Affirmations:

Action/Allowing:

Questions I Still Have:

Gratitude and Closing:

Invitation to Infinite Spiritual Team:	Date: / /

Intention:

Question:

```
                    4.
              Me Now/ How I'm
           Showing Up in the World



    3.                                    1.
  Manifestation/Flow              New Beginnings/
                                      Creation



                    2.
              My Strength/Power
```

Takeaways:
1.

2.

3.

4.

Affirmations:

Action/Allowing:

Questions I Still Have:

Gratitude and Closing:

"It's a funny thing about life, once you begin to take note of the things you are grateful for, you begin to lose sight of the things that you lack."

—Germany Kent

Invitation to Infinite Spiritual Team:	Date: / /

Intention:

Question:

```
                    4.
              ┌──────────────┐
              │   Me Now/ How I'm   │
              │ Showing Up in the World │
              └──────────────┘

                     ↑
       3.            │            1.
  ┌──────────┐   ♥   ┌──────────────┐
  │Manifestation/Flow│←─────→│ New Beginnings/ │
  └──────────┘       │    Creation     │
                     │   └──────────────┘
                     ↓
                    2.
              ┌──────────────┐
              │  My Strength/Power │
              └──────────────┘
```

Takeaways:
1.

2.

3.

4.

Affirmations:

Action/Allowing:

Questions I Still Have:

Gratitude and Closing:

Invitation to Infinite Spiritual Team:	Date: / /

Intention:

Question:

```
                    4.
              Me Now/ How I'm
           Showing Up in the World

    3.                                      1.
Manifestation/Flow                    New Beginnings/
                                         Creation

                    2.
              My Strength/Power
```

Takeaways:
1.

2.

3.

4.

Affirmations:

Action/Allowing:

Questions I Still Have:

Gratitude and Closing:

"Every day we are engaged in a miracle which we don't even recognize: a blue sky, white clouds, green leaves, the black, curious eyes of a child—our own two eyes. All is a miracle."

—Thich Nhat Hanh

Invitation to Infinite Spiritual Team:	Date: / /

Intention:

Question:

- 4. Me Now/ How I'm Showing Up in the World
- 1. New Beginnings/ Creation
- 2. My Strength/ Power
- 3. Manifestation/ Flow

Takeaways:
1.

2.

3.

4.

Affirmations:

Action/Allowing:

Questions I Still Have:

Gratitude and Closing:

Invitation to Infinite Spiritual Team:	Date: / /

Intention:

Question:

```
                    4.
              ┌─────────────┐
              │  Me Now/ How I'm │
              │ Showing Up in the World │
              └─────────────┘
                    ↑
        3.          │          1.
  ┌──────────┐    ♥    ┌──────────┐
  │ Manifestation/Flow │ ← → │ New Beginnings/ │
  │          │    │    │   Creation   │
  └──────────┘    ↓    └──────────┘
                    2.
              ┌─────────────┐
              │ My Strength/Power │
              └─────────────┘
```

Takeaways:
1.

2.

3.

4.

Affirmations:

Action/Allowing:

Questions I Still Have:

Gratitude and Closing:

"The strongest single factor in prosperity consciousness is self-esteem: believing you deserve it, believing you will get it."

—Jerry Gillies

Invitation to Infinite Spiritual Team:	Date: / /

Intention:

Question:

- 4. Me Now/ How I'm Showing Up in the World
- 1. New Beginnings/ Creation
- 2. My Strength/Power
- 3. Manifestation/Flow

Takeaways:
1.

2.

3.

4.

Affirmations:

Action/Allowing:

Questions I Still Have:

Gratitude and Closing:

Invitation to Infinite Spiritual Team:	Date: / /

Intention:

Question:

```
                    4.
              Me Now/ How I'm
            Showing Up in the World

                    ↑
  3.                                      1.
Manifestation/Flow  ← ♡ →       New Beginnings/
                                          Creation
                    ↓

                    2.
              My Strength/Power
```

Takeaways:
1.

2.

3.

4.

Affirmations:

Action/Allowing:

Questions I Still Have:

Gratitude and Closing:

"Try to be a good audience for whatever kind of experience reveals itself to you."

—Gary Thorp

Invitation to Infinite Spiritual Team:	Date: / /

Intention:

Question:

```
         4.
    Me Now/ How I'm
   Showing Up in the World

3.                                1.
Manifestation/Flow          New Beginnings/
                                Creation

         2.
    My Strength/Power
```

Takeaways:
1.

2.

3.

4.

Affirmations:

Action/Allowing:

Questions I Still Have:

Gratitude and Closing:

Invitation to Infinite Spiritual Team:	Date: / /

Intention:

Question:

```
                    4.
              ┌─────────────┐
              │  Me Now/ How I'm  │
              │ Showing Up in the World │
              └─────────────┘
                     ↑
        ┌────────────┼────────────┐
    3.  │            ♥            │  1.
   ┌─────┐ ←─────────┼─────────→ ┌─────┐
   │Manifestation/Flow│          │New Beginnings/│
   └─────┘            ↓          │   Creation    │
        └────────────┼────────────┘ └─────┘
                     ↓
              ┌─────────────┐
              │     2.      │
              │ My Strength/Power │
              └─────────────┘
```

Takeaways:

1.

2.

3.

4.

Affirmations:

Action/Allowing:

Questions I Still Have:

Gratitude and Closing:

"Love alone is what shows you the face of God. It's what offers you a home in the universe. It's what makes the stars shine."

—Belden C. Lane

Invitation to Infinite Spiritual Team:	Date: / /

Intention:

Question:

```
                    4.
            ┌─────────────────┐
            │   Me Now/ How I'm   │
            │ Showing Up in the World │
            └─────────────────┘

  3.                  ↑                    1.
┌──────────────┐     │      ┌──────────────┐
│ Manifestation/ │ ← ♡ →   │ New Beginnings/ │
│     Flow     │     │      │    Creation    │
└──────────────┘     ↓      └──────────────┘

                    2.
            ┌─────────────────┐
            │ My Strength/Power │
            └─────────────────┘
```

Takeaways:
1.

2.

3.

4.

Affirmations:

Action/Allowing:

Questions I Still Have:

Gratitude and Closing:

NOTES

| Invitation to Infinite Spiritual Team: | Date: / / |

Intention:

Question:

```
                    4.
              ┌───────────────┐
              │  Me Now/ How I'm │
              │ Showing Up in the World │
              └───────────────┘
                     ↑
   3.                │                1.
┌──────────────┐    ♡    ┌──────────────┐
│ Manifestation/Flow │←───┼───→│ New Beginnings/ │
└──────────────┘    │         │   Creation    │
                     ↓         └──────────────┘
                    2.
              ┌───────────────┐
              │ My Strength/Power │
              └───────────────┘
```

Takeaways:
1.

2.

3.

4.

Affirmations:

Action/Allowing:

Questions I Still Have:

Gratitude and Closing:

*"Angels are all around us, all the time,
in the very air we breathe."*

—Eileen Elias Freeman

Invitation to Infinite Spiritual Team:	Date: / /

Intention:

Question:

```
                    4.
              ┌──────────────┐
              │  Me Now/ How I'm │
              │ Showing Up in the World │
              └──────────────┘
                      ↑
  3.                  │                  1.
┌──────────────┐  ←── ♥ ──→  ┌──────────────┐
│ Manifestation/Flow │         │  New Beginnings/ │
└──────────────┘      │         │     Creation    │
                      ↓         └──────────────┘
              ┌──────────────┐
              │      2.      │
              │ My Strength/Power │
              └──────────────┘
```

Takeaways:
1.

2.

3.

4.

Affirmations:

Action/Allowing:

Questions I Still Have:

Gratitude and Closing:

Invitation to Infinite Spiritual Team:	Date: / /

Intention:

Question:

```
        4.
    Me Now/ How I'm
   Showing Up in the World

3.                                    1.
Manifestation/Flow          New Beginnings/
                                Creation

        2.
    My Strength/Power
```

Takeaways:
1.

2.

3.

4.

Affirmations:

Action/Allowing:

Questions I Still Have:

Gratitude and Closing:

*"Let yourself be silently drawn by
the strange pull of what you really love.
It will not lead you astray."*

—Rumi

Invitation to Infinite Spiritual Team:	Date: / /

Intention:

Question:

```
         4.
    Me Now/ How I'm
   Showing Up in the World


  3.                              1.
Manifestation/Flow          New Beginnings/
                               Creation


         2.
    My Strength/Power
```

Takeaways:
1.

2.

3.

4.

Affirmations:

Action/Allowing:

Questions I Still Have:

Gratitude and Closing:

Invitation to Infinite Spiritual Team:	Date: / /

Intention:

Question:

- 1. New Beginnings/ Creation
- 2. My Strength/Power
- 3. Manifestation/Flow
- 4. Me Now/ How I'm Showing Up in the World

Takeaways:
1.

2.

3.

4.

Affirmations:

Action/Allowing:

Questions I Still Have:

Gratitude and Closing:

*"True guidance is like a small torch in a dark forest. It
doesn't show everything once.
But gives enough light for the next step to be safe."*

—Swami Vivekanand

Invitation to Infinite Spiritual Team:	Date: / /

Intention:

Question:

```
                    4.
              ┌──────────────┐
              │  Me Now/ How I'm │
              │ Showing Up in the World │
              └──────────────┘
                     ↑
    3.               │              1.
┌──────────────┐  ← ♥ →  ┌──────────────┐
│ Manifestation/Flow │         │ New Beginnings/ │
└──────────────┘         │    Creation     │
                     ↓    └──────────────┘
              ┌──────────────┐
              │       2.       │
              │ My Strength/Power │
              └──────────────┘
```

Takeaways:
1.

2.

3.

4.

Affirmations:

Action/Allowing:

Questions I Still Have:

Gratitude and Closing:

| Invitation to Infinite Spiritual Team: | Date: / / |

Intention:

Question:

```
        4.
   Me Now/ How I'm
  Showing Up in the World

3.                          1.
Manifestation/Flow    New Beginnings/
                         Creation

        2.
   My Strength/Power
```

Takeaways:
1.

2.

3.

4.

Affirmations:

Action/Allowing:

Questions I Still Have:

Gratitude and Closing:

*"The secret of happiness is freedom,
the secret of freedom is courage."*

—Carrie Jones

Invitation to Infinite Spiritual Team:	Date: / /

Intention:

Question:

```
              4.
         Me Now/ How I'm
       Showing Up in the World

  3.                              1.
Manifestation/Flow          New Beginnings/
                                Creation

              2.
         My Strength/Power
```

Takeaways:
1.

2.

3.

4.

Affirmations:

Action/Allowing:

Questions I Still Have:

Gratitude and Closing:

| Invitation to Infinite Spiritual Team: | Date: / / |

Intention:

Question:

```
                    4.
              ┌──────────────┐
              │   Me Now/ How I'm    │
              │ Showing Up in the World │
              └──────────────┘

   3.                                      1.
┌──────────────┐                      ┌──────────────┐
│ Manifestation/Flow │                │  New Beginnings/  │
└──────────────┘                      │     Creation      │
                                      └──────────────┘

                    2.
              ┌──────────────┐
              │ My Strength/Power │
              └──────────────┘
```

Takeaways:
1.

2.

3.

4.

Affirmations:

Action/Allowing:

Questions I Still Have:

Gratitude and Closing:

"Happiness cannot be traveled to, owned, earned, worn or consumed. Happiness is the spiritual experience of living every minute with love, grace, and gratitude."

—Denis Waitley

| Invitation to Infinite Spiritual Team: | Date: / / |

Intention:

Question:

```
                    4.
              Me Now/ How I'm
             Showing Up in the World

    3.                    ♥              1.
Manifestation/Flow              New Beginnings/
                                   Creation

                    2.
              My Strength/Power
```

Takeaways:
1.

2.

3.

4.

Affirmations:

Action/Allowing:

Questions I Still Have:

Gratitude and Closing:

Invitation to Infinite Spiritual Team:	Date: / /

Intention:

Question:

- 4. Me Now/ How I'm Showing Up in the World
- 1. New Beginnings/ Creation
- 2. My Strength/Power
- 3. Manifestation/Flow

Takeaways:
1.

2.

3.

4.

Affirmations:

Action/Allowing:

Questions I Still Have:

Gratitude and Closing:

*"Find a place inside where there's joy,
and the joy will burn out the pain."*

—Joseph Campbell

Invitation to Infinite Spiritual Team:	Date: / /

Intention:

Question:

- 4. Me Now / How I'm Showing Up in the World
- 1. New Beginnings / Creation
- 2. My Strength / Power
- 3. Manifestation / Flow

Takeaways:
1.

2.

3.

4.

Affirmations:

Action/Allowing:

Questions I Still Have:

Gratitude and Closing:

Invitation to Infinite Spiritual Team:	Date: / /

Intention:

Question:

- 4. Me Now/ How I'm Showing Up in the World
- 3. Manifestation/Flow
- 1. New Beginnings/Creation
- 2. My Strength/Power

Takeaways:
1.

2.

3.

4.

Affirmations:

Action/Allowing:

Questions I Still Have:

Gratitude and Closing:

*"Remember there's no such thing
as a small act of kindness.
Every act creates a ripple with no logical end."*

—Scott Adams

Invitation to Infinite Spiritual Team:	Date: / /

Intention:

Question:

```
                    4.
              ┌──────────────┐
              │  Me Now/ How I'm │
              │ Showing Up in the World │
              └──────────────┘

   3.                                          1.
┌──────────────┐                         ┌──────────────┐
│ Manifestation/Flow │  ←  ♡  →           │ New Beginnings/ │
└──────────────┘                         │    Creation    │
                                         └──────────────┘

                    2.
              ┌──────────────┐
              │ My Strength/Power │
              └──────────────┘
```

Takeaways:

1.

2.

3.

4.

Affirmations:

Action/Allowing:

Questions I Still Have:

Gratitude and Closing:

Invitation to Infinite Spiritual Team:	Date: / /

Intention:

Question:

```
                    4.
              Me Now/ How I'm
           Showing Up in the World

                     ↑
                     |
  3.          ←    ♥    →          1.
Manifestation/Flow                New Beginnings/
                     |             Creation
                     ↓

                    2.
              My Strength/Power
```

Takeaways:
1.

2.

3.

4.

Affirmations:

Action/Allowing:

Questions I Still Have:

Gratitude and Closing:

"A generous person will prosper."

—Proverbs 11:25

| Invitation to Infinite Spiritual Team: | Date: /   / |

Intention:

Question:

- 4. Me Now/ How I'm Showing Up in the World
- 1. New Beginnings/ Creation
- 2. My Strength/Power
- 3. Manifestation/Flow

Takeaways:
1.

2.

3.

4.

Affirmations:

Action/Allowing:

Questions I Still Have:

Gratitude and Closing:

| Invitation to Infinite Spiritual Team: | Date: /   / |

Intention:

Question:

- 4. Me Now / How I'm Showing Up in the World
- 1. New Beginnings / Creation
- 2. My Strength / Power
- 3. Manifestation / Flow

Takeaways:
1.

2.

3.

4.

Affirmations:

Action/Allowing:

Questions I Still Have:

Gratitude and Closing:

"And, when you want something, all the universe conspires in helping you to achieve it."

—Paulo Coelho

Invitation to Infinite Spiritual Team:	Date: / /

Intention:

Question:

```
                    4.
              Me Now/ How I'm
            Showing Up in the World

    3.                                    1.
Manifestation/Flow                   New Beginnings/
                                        Creation

                    2.
              My Strength/Power
```

Takeaways:
1.

2.

3.

4.

Affirmations:

Action/Allowing:

Questions I Still Have:

Gratitude and Closing:

NOTES

Invitation to Infinite Spiritual Team:	Date: / /

Intention:

Question:

- 4. Me Now/ How I'm Showing Up in the World
- 1. New Beginnings/ Creation
- 2. My Strength/Power
- 3. Manifestation/Flow

Takeaways:
1.

2.

3.

4.

Affirmations:

Action/Allowing:

Questions I Still Have:

Gratitude and Closing:

"Don't dismiss the synchronicity of what is happening right now finding its way to your life at just this moment. There are no coincidences in the universe, only convergences of Will, Intent, and Experience."

—Neale Donald Walsch

Invitation to Infinite Spiritual Team:	Date: / /

Intention:

Question:

```
            4.
     Me Now/ How I'm
    Showing Up in the World

                ↑
3.         ←  ♡  →         1.
Manifestation/Flow        New Beginnings/
                ↓          Creation

            2.
      My Strength/Power
```

Takeaways:
1.

2.

3.

4.

Affirmations:

Action/Allowing:

Questions I Still Have:

Gratitude and Closing:

| Invitation to Infinite Spiritual Team: | Date: / / |

Intention:

Question:

- 4. Me Now / How I'm Showing Up in the World
- 3. Manifestation/Flow
- 1. New Beginnings/Creation
- 2. My Strength/Power

Takeaways:
1.

2.

3.

4.

Affirmations:

Action/Allowing:

Questions I Still Have:

Gratitude and Closing:

"Abundance is not something we acquire. It is something we tune into."

—Wayne Dyer

Invitation to Infinite Spiritual Team:	Date: / /

Intention:

Question:

```
         4.
    Me Now/ How I'm
   Showing Up in the World


3.                              1.
Manifestation/Flow          New Beginnings/
                                Creation


         2.
    My Strength/Power
```

Takeaways:
1.

2.

3.

4.

Affirmations:

Action/Allowing:

Questions I Still Have:

Gratitude and Closing:

Invitation to Infinite Spiritual Team:	Date: / /

Intention:

Question:

- 4. Me Now/ How I'm Showing Up in the World
- 1. New Beginnings/ Creation
- 2. My Strength/Power
- 3. Manifestation/Flow

Takeaways:
1.

2.

3.

4.

Affirmations:

Action/Allowing:

Questions I Still Have:

Gratitude and Closing:

"All that we are is the result of what we have thought.

—Buddha

Invitation to Infinite Spiritual Team:	Date: / /

Intention:

Question:

```
            4.
       Me Now/ How I'm
    Showing Up in the World


  3.                              1.
Manifestation/Flow          New Beginnings/
                               Creation

            2.
       My Strength/Power
```

Takeaways:
1.

2.

3.

4.

Affirmations:

Action/Allowing:

Questions I Still Have:

Gratitude and Closing:

| Invitation to Infinite Spiritual Team: | Date: / / |

Intention:

Question:

- 4. Me Now/ How I'm Showing Up in the World
- 1. New Beginnings/ Creation
- 2. My Strength/Power
- 3. Manifestation/Flow

Takeaways:
1.

2.

3.

4.

Affirmations:

Action/Allowing:

Questions I Still Have:

Gratitude and Closing:

"The successful warrior is the average man, with laser-like focus."

—Bruce Lee

Invitation to Infinite Spiritual Team:	Date: / /
Intention:	
Question:	

```
                        4.
                   Me Now/ How I'm
                 Showing Up in the World

        3.                    ♥                    1.
   Manifestation/Flow                          New Beginnings/
                                                  Creation

                        2.
                   My Strength/Power
```

Takeaways:
1.

2.

3.

4.

Affirmations:

Action/Allowing:

Questions I Still Have:

Gratitude and Closing:

| Invitation to Infinite Spiritual Team: | Date: /   / |

Intention:

Question:

```
                    4.
              Me Now/ How I'm
            Showing Up in the World


    3.                                    1.
Manifestation/Flow                  New Beginnings/
                                        Creation


                    2.
              My Strength/Power
```

Takeaways:
1.

2.

3.

4.

Affirmations:

Action/Allowing:

Questions I Still Have:

Gratitude and Closing:

*"Be kind whenever possible.
It is always possible.*

—Dalai Lama

Invitation to Infinite Spiritual Team:	Date: / /

Intention:

Question:

```
                    4.
            ┌─────────────────┐
            │   Me Now/ How I'm   │
            │ Showing Up in the World │
            └─────────────────┘
                     ↑
   3.                │              1.
┌──────────┐        ♥         ┌──────────┐
│ Manifestation/ │ ← ─ ─ ─ → │ New Beginnings/ │
│    Flow       │              │    Creation     │
└──────────┘        │         └──────────┘
                     ↓
            ┌─────────────────┐
            │                 │
            │  My Strength/Power │
            └─────────────────┘
                    2.
```

Takeaways:

1.

2.

3.

4.

Affirmations:

Action/Allowing:

Questions I Still Have:

Gratitude and Closing:

NOTES

Invitation to Infinite Spiritual Team:	Date: / /

Intention:

Question:

```
         4.
    Me Now/ How I'm
   Showing Up in the World


  3.                              1.
Manifestation/Flow          New Beginnings/
                                Creation


         2.
    My Strength/Power
```

Takeaways:
1.

2.

3.

4.

Affirmations:

Action/Allowing:

Questions I Still Have:

Gratitude and Closing:

"It always seems impossible until it's done."

—Nelson Mandela

Invitation to Infinite Spiritual Team:	**Date:** / /

Intention:

Question:

```
                    4.
              Me Now / How I'm
           Showing Up in the World

    3.                                    1.
Manifestation/Flow              New Beginnings/
                                    Creation

                    2.
              My Strength/Power
```

Takeaways:
1.

2.

3.

4.

Affirmations:

Action/Allowing:

Questions I Still Have:

Gratitude and Closing:

Invitation to Infinite Spiritual Team:	Date: / /

Intention:

Question:

```
        4.
   Me Now/ How I'm
  Showing Up in the World

3.                                    1.
Manifestation/Flow         New Beginnings/
                                 Creation

        2.
   My Strength/Power
```

Takeaways:
1.

2.

3.

4.

Affirmations:

Action/Allowing:

Questions I Still Have:

Gratitude and Closing:

*"Try not to become a person of success,
but rather to become a person of value."*

—Albert Einstein

Invitation to Infinite Spiritual Team:	Date: / /

Intention:

Question:

1. New Beginnings/Creation
2. My Strength/Power
3. Manifestation/Flow
4. Me Now/ How I'm Showing Up in the World

Takeaways:
1.

2.

3.

4.

Affirmations:

Action/Allowing:

Questions I Still Have:

Gratitude and Closing:

| Invitation to Infinite Spiritual Team: | Date: / / |

Intention:

Question:

```
                    4.
              Me Now/ How I'm
            Showing Up in the World


    3.                                    1.
Manifestation/Flow                 New Beginnings/
                                       Creation


                    2.
              My Strength/Power
```

Takeaways:
1.

2.

3.

4.

Affirmations:

Action/Allowing:

Questions I Still Have:

Gratitude and Closing:

"Turn your wounds into wisdom."

—Oprah Winfrey

Invitation to Infinite Spiritual Team:	Date: / /

Intention:

Question:

- 4. Me Now/ How I'm Showing Up in the World
- 1. New Beginnings/ Creation
- 2. My Strength/Power
- 3. Manifestation/Flow

Takeaways:
1.

2.

3.

4.

Affirmations:

Action/Allowing:

Questions I Still Have:

Gratitude and Closing:

Invitation to Infinite Spiritual Team:	Date: / /

Intention:

Question:

```
            4.
    ┌──────────────┐
    │ Me Now/ How I'm │
    │ Showing Up in the World │
    └──────────────┘
            ↑
3.          │          1.
┌──────────┐  ♥  ┌──────────┐
│Manifestation/│←─┼─→│New Beginnings/│
│    Flow    │     │   Creation   │
└──────────┘     └──────────┘
            ↓
            2.
    ┌──────────────┐
    │ My Strength/Power │
    └──────────────┘
```

Takeaways:
1.

2.

3.

4.

Affirmations:

Action/Allowing:

Questions I Still Have:

Gratitude and Closing:

"Do what you can, with what you have, where you are."

—Theodore Roosevelt

Invitation to Infinite Spiritual Team:	Date: / /

Intention:

Question:

```
            4.
      Me Now/ How I'm
    Showing Up in the World

3.                              1.
Manifestation/Flow      New Beginnings/
                              Creation

            2.
      My Strength/Power
```

Takeaways:
1.

2.

3.

4.

Affirmations:

Action/Allowing:

Questions I Still Have:

Gratitude and Closing:

Invitation to Infinite Spiritual Team:	Date: / /

Intention:

Question:

1. New Beginnings/Creation
2. My Strength/Power
3. Manifestation/Flow
4. Me Now/ How I'm Showing Up in the World

Takeaways:
1.

2.

3.

4.

Affirmations:

Action/Allowing:

Questions I Still Have:

Gratitude and Closing:

"Love the life you live. Live the life you love."

—Bob Marley

www.ingramcontent.com/pod-product-compliance
Lightning Source LLC
Chambersburg PA
CBHW020905080526
44589CB00011B/453